A BUSINESS APPROACH TO TOMATO FARMING

Complete Entrepreneurial Step By Step Guide To Tomato Garden From Scratch

ZHURI HART

DISCLAIMER

This book is intended to provide general information and insights on adopting a business approach to farming. The content within is based on the author's knowledge and experiences up to the date of publication. It is essential to recognize that the field of agriculture is dynamic, influenced by various factors such as market conditions, climate, and regulatory changes.

Readers are advised to conduct thorough research, seek professional advice, and consider their unique circumstances before implementing any strategies or practices discussed in this book. The author and publisher disclaim any responsibility for the accuracy, completeness, or suitability of the information provided. The book is not a substitute for professional advice, and the author and publisher shall not be liable for any damages or losses arising from the use or reliance on the information presented herein.

Individual results may vary, and success in farming enterprises is contingent upon numerous variables. The author encourages readers to consult with relevant experts, agricultural extension services, and legal or financial professionals to tailor strategies to their specific needs and local conditions.

This book is not intended to be a comprehensive guide to all aspects of farming, and readers should exercise their judgment and discretion in applying the principles discussed. The author and publisher do not endorse any specific products, services, or companies mentioned in this book unless explicitly stated.

By reading this book, the reader acknowledges and accepts the inherent uncertainties in agricultural endeavors and agrees to use the information at their own risk.

TABLE OF CONTENTS

CHAPTER ONE 13

TOMATO FARMING INTRODUCTION...............................13

WHY GROW TOMATOES?...13

THE VIEWPOINT OF BUSINESS 14

CHAPTER TWO 17

KNOWING THE MARKET FOR TOMATOES........................17

AN OUTLINE OF THE TOMATO BUSINESS.......................17

ANALYSIS OF DEMAND AND MARKET TRENDS 17

FINDING THE RIGHT TARGET MARKETS 18

COMPARATIVE EVALUATION 19

PROSPECTS AND DIFFICULTIES....................................19

CHAPTER THREE 21

HOW TO BEGIN GROWING TOMATOES 21

CHOOSING THE PROPER TYPES OF TOMATOES 21

PLANNING FOR CROPS AND SOIL PREPARATION 21

CLIMATE AND ENVIRONMENTAL FACTORS TO TAKE INTO 22

SOURCING SEEDS AND ENSURING QUALITY 23

INFRASTRUCTURE AND EQUIPMENT 24

CHAPTER FOUR 25

METHODS OF CULTIVATION...25

PLANTING AND TRANSPLANTING..................................25

IRRIGATION SYSTEMS..25

FERTILIZATION PRACTICES 26

CROP ROTATION AND SUSTAINABLE PRACTICES 28

CHAPTER FIVE...29

  HARVESTING AND MANAGING AFTER HARVEST...............29

    CALCULATING THE IDEAL HARVEST TIME 29

    METHODS OF HARVESTING......................................30

    CLASSIFYING AND RATING 30

    TRANSPORTATION AND STORAGE 31

    MEASURES FOR QUALITY CONTROL.........................32

CHAPTER SIX..33

  BUDGETING AND FINANCIAL PLANNING 33

    CALCULATING LAUNCH COSTS 33

    RETURN ON INVESTMENT ANALYSIS.......................34

    MANAGING FINANCES EFFECTIVELY 35

CHAPTER SEVEN 37

  MARKETING PLANS FOR ESTABLISHING YOUR TOMATO COMPANY BRAND..37

    MAKING A STRATEGY FOR MARKETING.....................37

    USING OFFLINE AND ONLINE CHANNELS...................38

    DEVELOPING CONNECTIONS WITH PURCHASERS...........39

    MARKETING TECHNIQUES......................................39

CHAPTER EIGHT...41

  REGULATORY AND LEGAL ASPECTS..............................41

    COMPREHENDING AGRICULTURAL REGULATIONS 41

    LICENSES AND PERMITS 41

    ADHERENCE TO ENVIRONMENTAL GUIDELINES 42

    RISK MANAGEMENT AND INSURANCE.....................43

FARMERS' LEGAL PROTECTIONS 43

CHAPTER NINE 45

CASE STUDIES AND STORIES OF TRIUMPH...........................45

ANALYZING PROFITABLE TOMATO FARMING ENTERPRISES.............45

ACQUIRING KNOWLEDGE FROM OBSTACLES AND SETBACKS 46

MODIFYING TECHNIQUES FOR VARIOUS LOCATIONS.......................47

CONVERSATIONS WITH SKILLED TOMATO GROWERS 48

ABOUT THE BOOK

"A Business Approach to Tomato Farming," a thorough manual, is an invaluable tool for anyone hoping to get into the tomato farming business or grow an existing one. This book aims to close the gap between conventional farming methods and modern business strategies, stressing the significance of an all-encompassing strategy for long-term success.

Why Grow Tomatoes? Given the substantial worldwide need for this adaptable product, the decision to concentrate on tomato growing was well thought out. The book shows how a strategic business approach may turn a tomato farm into a successful business by examining the particular opportunities and problems faced by the tomato sector.

The Business Perspective: This guide looks at every facet of tomato farming from the perspective of business, including everything from financial planning and marketing tactics to market analysis and cultivation methods.

Readers may create a solid framework for making wise judgments and streamlining their operations by using business ideas.

A wide range of people are interested in this book, including entrepreneurs who want to invest in the agricultural industry, seasoned growers who want to increase productivity, and new farmers who want to launch their tomato farms. Both novices and seasoned professionals can easily understand the text, which offers insightful information for all skill levels.

The book is organized to lead readers through a logical progression, beginning with an examination of the tomato market and ending with case studies and success stories from actual businesses. Every chapter builds on the one before it, forming a seamless story that gives readers the information and abilities they need to succeed in tomato farming.

The book explore important facets of growing tomatoes. The dynamics of the tomato market are examined along with trends, demand and target market analysis, competitive analysis, and possible possibilities and obstacles. Initiating a tomato farm is made easier by the practical advice, which covers topics including variety selection, soil preparation, climate concerns, seed sources, and infrastructure.

Cultivation methods, including planting, irrigation, fertilizer, pest control, and post-harvest procedures, are covered in detail. The book discusses financial planning and budgeting, including funding, return on investment analysis, yearly budgeting, startup costs, and efficient financial management. Building strong marketing strategies is the main topic, which also covers branding, marketing strategy, buyer relationships, online and offline platforms, and promotional techniques.

The book covers agricultural rules, permits, environmental compliance, insurance, and legal protections for farmers. It also discusses legal and regulatory matters. Ultimately, the book offers insightful case studies and success stories that give a realistic perspective on the difficulties, setbacks, and flexibility needed for success in many areas.

"A Business Approach to Tomato Farming" is an important resource that offers a thorough and useful road map for anyone wishing to approach the challenges of tomato growing from a business-oriented perspective.

CHAPTER ONE

TOMATO FARMING INTRODUCTION

WHY GROW TOMATOES?

Particularly important to modern agriculture is the production of tomatoes, which combines economic feasibility, nutritional value, and ecological sustainability. The versatility of this agricultural endeavor in the gastronomic, nutritional, and commercial realms has led to its rise in importance on a global scale, spanning geographical boundaries. Tomato production is more than just a conventional agricultural method; it's a vibrant, ever-evolving industry that combines commerce, science, and technology.

The decision to start a tomato farm is frequently motivated by the crop's diverse appeal. Nutritionally speaking, tomatoes are abundant in vital vitamins, minerals, and antioxidants that support a diet that is well-balanced and wholesome.

Their versatility as a basic ingredient across many cuisines further establishes their significance in the world's culinary traditions. But beyond the kitchen, tomato farming has become a major commercial venture that propels the tomato farming sector from a business standpoint.

Tomato growing has a wide range of commercial prospects and difficulties. Tomatoes are in high demand outside of homes; they are used in food processing, canning, and restaurant businesses. Tomatoes and other fresh, locally sourced produce are in high demand as customer preferences shift toward healthier and more sustainable options. Because of this change in consumer behavior, tomato cultivation is becoming more and more appealing to those interested in agribusiness.

THE VIEWPOINT OF BUSINESS

Growing and harvesting tomatoes is only one aspect of tomato farming from an economic standpoint. It entails strategic deliberations about supply chain logistics, market dynamics, and technology integration. To maintain a successful and long-lasting business model, entrepreneurs in the tomato farming industry must manage the intricacies of pricing swings, weather-related hazards, and market trends.

Tomato growing not only has economic potential, but it also creates jobs and promotes rural development. Since tomatoes require a lot of labor, growing them frequently involves the involvement of local communities, which opens up opportunities for skill development and revenue generation.

This socio-economic component emphasizes even more how important tomato production is as a comprehensive industry that goes beyond simple farming methods.

There are a variety of ecological, dietary, and financial factors that go into growing tomatoes. Whether considered in terms of gastronomic pleasure, nutritional value, or business prospects, tomato farming is shown to be a dynamic and essential part of contemporary agriculture. This introduction provides context for a thorough examination of the many aspects of tomato farming and sheds light on its importance from a business and global standpoint.

CHAPTER TWO

KNOWING THE MARKET FOR TOMATOES

AN OUTLINE OF THE TOMATO BUSINESS

The tomato is a major economic commodity and a staple in diets worldwide, making it an important part of the agricultural landscape. Tomatoes are a highly versatile food that can be used in many different ways. They can be consumed raw, processed (such as sauces and canned goods), or as an ingredient in a wide range of recipes. A wide spectrum of stakeholders, from small-scale regional farmers to massive international agribusinesses, defines this industry. Tomatoes are cultivated all over the world, with different regions contributing to the total amount produced.

ANALYSIS OF DEMAND AND MARKET TRENDS

For those involved in the tomato industry, they must comprehend market trends and demand patterns.

Dietary practices and consumer preferences have a big impact on market dynamics. Fresh and organic tomatoes are in higher demand as a result of the growing trend toward healthier eating in recent years. Convenience and the desire for ready-to-use products have led to growth in the processed tomato product market. In addition, variables like population expansion, urbanization, and shifting lifestyles affect the total demand for tomatoes.

FINDING THE RIGHT TARGET MARKETS

Target market identification entails a careful examination of customer preferences, demographics, and geographic factors. Local markets and grocery stores should be the main destinations for fresh tomatoes, but supermarkets and internet retailers may be able to reach a wider audience with processed tomato products. Understanding international market preferences and regulatory requirements is essential, and export opportunities are also important. A strategic approach to maximize sales and market penetration can be achieved by targeting diverse markets according to product types and consumer behaviors.

COMPARATIVE EVALUATION

There is fierce competition among players in the tomato industry, which ranges from small-scale farmers to large multinational corporations. Distribution networks, branding, quality assurance, and production efficiency are important components that affect competitiveness. While larger companies concentrate on economies of scale and technological innovations, local farmers may compete on price and freshness. Comprehending the advantages and disadvantages of rivals, in addition to market positioning, helps stakeholders hone their tactics and secure a competitive advantage.

PROSPECTS AND DIFFICULTIES

Opportunities in the tomato industry are frequently associated with new developments in technology, consumer preferences, and emerging trends. For example, there are opportunities for farmers who adopt such practices because of the growing demand for tomatoes that are produced sustainably and organically. Developments in packaging and processing methods also create opportunities for new product creation. The industry does, however, have to contend with issues like production being negatively impacted by climate change, commodity prices fluctuating, and the requirement for environmentally friendly farming methods. To effectively navigate these challenges, industry participants must collaborate, invest in research and development, and make strategic plans.

A thorough comprehension of the tomato market necessitates examining its dynamics from a variety of perspectives, such as an industry overview, market trends, target markets, the competitive environment, and opportunities and challenges. Competently navigating these facets will put stakeholders in a better position to prosper in this vital and dynamic area of the agricultural economy.

CHAPTER THREE

HOW TO BEGIN GROWING TOMATOES

CHOOSING THE PROPER TYPES OF TOMATOES

A key component of successful tomato farming is selecting the right tomato varieties. The choice should be made taking into account the climate, kind of soil, and intended use of the tomatoes. While indeterminate varieties offer a longer harvest period, determinate varieties are best for those seeking a concentrated harvest. When choosing varieties, one should also take disease resistance, fruit size, and taste into account. Making educated decisions that are suited to their unique needs and circumstances can be aided by farmers conducting in-depth research and speaking with regional agricultural specialists.

PLANNING FOR CROPS AND SOIL PREPARATION

A healthy tomato crop requires careful soil preparation. To start, farmers should conduct tests on the soil to ascertain its composition, pH, and nutrient levels. Soils that drain well and have a pH of 6.0 to 6.8 are ideal for growing tomatoes. Compost and other organic matter should be added to the soil to improve its fertility and structure. Crop planning entails choosing the field's configuration, plant spacing, and crop arrangement as a whole. Proper air circulation is made possible by adequate spacing, which lowers the risk of illness. To stop soil-borne pathogens and pests from multiplying over several growing seasons, crop rotation is also advised.

CLIMATE AND ENVIRONMENTAL FACTORS TO TAKE INTO ACCOUNT

Because of their sensitivity to temperature changes, tomatoes require a thorough understanding of the local climate to be successfully cultivated. The majority of tomato cultivars prefer warm temperatures, ranging from 70°F to 80°F (21°C to 27°C). Tomato plants may suffer from frost, so growers should know when their area typically experiences frost and adjust their planting schedule accordingly. It's also critical to take into account environmental elements like wind and sun exposure. Good irrigation techniques, such as keeping an eye on water needs and steering clear of soggy ground, improve the general well-being of tomato plants.

SOURCING SEEDS AND ENSURING QUALITY

Purchasing top-notch seeds is essential to a profitable tomato farming endeavor. To guarantee genetic purity and dependability, farmers should purchase seeds from reliable vendors or accredited seed producers. Before planting, germination tests can be used to determine the viability of the seeds.

To sustain seed viability over time, quality assurance also entails following recommended seed storage practices. The overall efficiency of the farming operation can be increased by properly labeling and recording seed varieties to avoid confusion during planting and harvesting.

INFRASTRUCTURE AND EQUIPMENT

For effective tomato farming, the correct infrastructure and equipment must be purchased. This covers equipment for preparing soil, watering systems, and covering structures like tunnels or greenhouses. The equipment selection is based on the operation's size as well as the farm's particular requirements. For effective and regulated water distribution, tomatoes are frequently grown using drip irrigation systems. Longer growing seasons are made possible by greenhouses' shelter from pests and bad weather. To guarantee peak performance and lower the possibility of crop loss owing to mechanical problems, farmers should routinely maintain and calibrate their equipment. Having the right infrastructure also helps to make farming operations more efficient and well-organized.

CHAPTER FOUR

METHODS OF CULTIVATION

PLANTING AND TRANSPLANTING

These are critical phases in agricultural production that greatly impact a crop's ability to succeed. The timing and technique of planting have a big impact on the overall growth and yield of the plants. While transplanting entails the germination of seeds in controlled conditions before moving seedlings to the final planting site, direct seeding includes planting seeds directly into the soil. Every technique offers benefits and things to keep in mind, like crop kind, environment, and intended yield. By improving control over the initial phases of plant growth, transplanting ensures a more consistent and reliable crop.

IRRIGATION SYSTEMS

Providing crops with the appropriate moisture requires effective water management, which is mostly dependent on irrigation systems. There are many different irrigation techniques, and each has benefits and drawbacks of its own. For example, drip irrigation minimizes water waste and lowers the risk of illness by providing water directly to the base of plants. Sprinkler systems, on the other hand, disperse water throughout the whole crop area and are appropriate for specific crops and regions. The crop requirements, climate conditions in the area, and the availability of water all influence the irrigation system selection. Putting into practice sustainable irrigation techniques is essential for maintaining long-term agricultural profitability and preserving water supplies.

FERTILIZATION PRACTICES

Fertilization is a crucial part of gardening that entails giving plants the nutrients they need to grow as healthily as possible. Crop type, specific nutrient requirements, and soil fertility all influence the choice of fertilization techniques. While synthetic fertilizers offer a quicker boost to nutrients, organic fertilizers, which come from natural sources, support soil health and sustainability. Provisioning the proper amounts of trace elements, phosphorus, potassium, and nitrogen is known as balanced fertilization. With the use of precision agriculture tools, farmers can customize their fertilization strategies based on crop monitoring and soil testing, optimizing nutrient uptake and reducing environmental impact.

Agriculture faces a continuing struggle in managing pests and diseases, which calls for a proactive and coordinated strategy. Chemical interventions, cultural practices, and biological control are frequently used tactics to lessen the effects of illnesses and pests. The goal of integrated pest management, or IPM, is to control pests as much as possible while causing the least amount of harm to the environment. Using resistant crop varieties, rotating crops, and companion planting are examples of cultural approaches that break pest cycles. Sustainable and resilient agricultural systems are enhanced by effective pest and disease management, which requires regular monitoring, early diagnosis, and targeted treatments.

CROP ROTATION AND SUSTAINABLE PRACTICES

Using the same plot of land to grow various crops in successive seasons is known as crop rotation, and it is a sustainable agricultural technique. This method strengthens soil structure, promotes nutrient cycling, and breaks the cycles of disease and pests. Crop rotation with varying nutrient requirements keeps soil from being too thin and improves soil health in general. Agroecological techniques that emphasize ecological balance, biodiversity conservation, and low environmental impact are also included in sustainable farming practices. Examples of sustainable methods that work to preserve or improve soil health, lessen erosion, and increase overall ecosystem resilience are conservation tillage, cover crops, and agroforestry. Adopting such techniques ensures the health of the environment and the crops farmed, so contributing to the long-term sustainability of agriculture.

CHAPTER FIVE

HARVESTING AND MANAGING AFTER HARVEST

CALCULATING THE IDEAL HARVEST TIME

A critical component of agricultural techniques is determining the best time to harvest because it has a direct impact on the quantity and quality of the produce. To determine when to harvest, farmers and agricultural professionals use a combination of scientific techniques and traditional knowledge. Crop maturity, meteorological circumstances, and consumer demand are all important considerations in this decision-making process.

It is possible to determine whether crops are ready for harvest by keeping an eye on characteristics like color, size, and sugar content. Using cutting-edge technologies like predictive modeling and remote sensing improves the accuracy of when to harvest for maximum nutritional value and market appeal.

METHODS OF HARVESTING

Harvesting techniques are a collection of strategies used to collect crops effectively with the least amount of damage to the product. The type of crop and its unique qualities determine the best harvesting method. Hand harvesting is a frequent method used for fruits and vegetables that need to be handled carefully. It involves labor-intensive techniques. On the other hand, mechanized harvesting makes use of equipment like combine harvesters for large-scale grain crops. The process of choosing the right technique affects the overall success and efficiency of the harvest since it takes into account factors like crop type, labor availability, and cost-effectiveness.

CLASSIFYING AND RATING

A vital part of post-harvest management, sorting, and grading are essential in establishing the agricultural produce's market worth. Crops are sorted according to several factors, including size, color, and quality. By removing faulty or inferior products, this procedure helps guarantee that only the best goods are sold. Grading, on the other hand, makes pricing and marketing tactics easier by classifying the collected items into distinct quality levels. Sorting and grading both help to meet customer expectations, keep product quality consistent, and increase market competitiveness.

TRANSPORTATION AND STORAGE

From the field to the market, maintaining the quality and freshness of produced commodities depends heavily on efficient storage and transportation. Produce shelf life can be increased by using proper storage facilities, such as cold storage for perishables or controlled environment storage for some fruits. Furthermore, using the right packing supplies and methods helps to keep crops safe while in transit. The quality of the crop is preserved throughout the supply chain by using cold chains, refrigerated trucks, and other transportation techniques to maintain ideal temperature and humidity levels. Agricultural output must be transported and stored with optimal efficiency to reduce losses and maximize its economic value.

MEASURES FOR QUALITY CONTROL

To maintain the standards of the harvested crops, quality control procedures are put into place at different phases of post-harvest management. This entails constant testing, inspection, and monitoring to spot and address any deviations from the intended quality standards. Using technology for real-time monitoring, visual inspections, and laboratory testing to evaluate variables including moisture content, chemical composition, and general freshness are some examples of quality control methods. By putting quality control methods in place, agricultural producers and distributors not only guarantee that the final product satisfies regulatory standards but also improve consumer satisfaction, foster market trust, and develop their reputation.

CHAPTER SIX

BUDGETING AND FINANCIAL PLANNING

CALCULATING LAUNCH COSTS

A crucial part of any new venture's financial strategy is estimating launch costs. This entails determining and computing every cost related to starting a business, such as equipment, permits, licenses, initial inventory, marketing costs, and legal fees, among others.

A thorough assessment of beginning expenses gives business owners a realistic financial picture, enabling them to obtain the required capital and decide whether their venture is viable.

A crucial part of financial planning is annual budgeting, which is estimating income and expenses for a given time frame, usually a year. Businesses can define financial goals, analyze performance against those goals, and allocate resources efficiently thanks to this procedure.

Organizations can prioritize spending, find areas for cost savings, and adjust to shifting market conditions through annual budgeting. It helps to maintain financial discipline throughout the fiscal year and acts as a roadmap for financial decision-making.

RETURN ON INVESTMENT ANALYSIS

An essential financial indicator, return on investment (ROI) analysis assesses an investment's profitability about its cost. Businesses must evaluate the possible return on investments or projects to make well-informed decisions.

Organizations can prioritize initiatives with higher return on investment (ROI), optimize resource allocation, and improve overall financial performance by comparing the predicted gains against the initial investment. ROI analysis is a crucial tool for strategic decision-making, assisting companies in concentrating on projects with the biggest potential financial returns.

Obtaining Funds and Grants: For both new and existing companies, obtaining funds and grants is a critical component of financial planning. To pay for expansion goals, working capital needs, or beginning fees, entrepreneurs frequently look outside for investment. This may entail looking for investors, applying for grants from public or private institutions, or getting loans. Finding the best funding sources, comprehending their terms and conditions, and building a strong case to secure the required financial help are all essential components of successful financial planning.

MANAGING FINANCES EFFECTIVELY

Any business's long-term viability and success depend on its ability to manage its finances. This entails putting in place reliable financial controls, keeping an eye on cash flow, and keeping correct financial records. Companies must set up and follow budgets, evaluate their financial accounts regularly, and modify their plans in response to their financial performance. To ensure the organization's resilience in changeable business contexts, effective financial management also entails contingency planning for unanticipated occurrences, such as economic downturns or unexpected expenses.

Budgeting and financial planning are essential elements of strategic business management. A complete and long-lasting financial plan for businesses of all sizes is facilitated by interrelated procedures such as estimating launch expenses, yearly budgeting, ROI analysis, obtaining funds and grants, and efficiently managing cash.

CHAPTER SEVEN

MARKETING PLANS FOR ESTABLISHING YOUR TOMATO COMPANY BRAND

Any business, even one that sells tomatoes, must build a strong brand to succeed. Beyond designing a catchy logo, branding is developing a unique identity that appeals to your target market. This can entail stressing aspects like sustainability, freshness, and quality for a tomato company. Think about creating a distinctive brand narrative that highlights the care and attention that goes into each step of your tomato's journey, from seed to harvest.

MAKING A STRATEGY FOR MARKETING

An effective marketing strategy is the road map that leads your company to success. To begin, thoroughly investigate the market to gain insight into your target market and rivals. Determine your tomato business's main advantages and points of differentiation, then list your precise marketing goals.

Both short- and long-term tactics, such as product positioning, price, distribution routes, and promotional activities, should be included in your plan. Review and modify your marketing strategy frequently to keep up with shifting market conditions.

USING OFFLINE AND ONLINE CHANNELS

In the era of digitalization, a successful marketing plan incorporates both offline and online channels. Having a strong online presence is crucial, which should include an easy-to-use website, active social media accounts, and maybe even e-commerce features.

To reach a larger audience, make use of digital marketing tools like social media advertising and search engine optimization (SEO). In addition, don't undervalue the effectiveness of conventional offline channels like working with grocery shops, attending neighborhood farmers' markets, and handing out flyers or business cards.

DEVELOPING CONNECTIONS WITH PURCHASERS

Effective marketing relies heavily on establishing trusting connections with consumers. This entails knowing the requirements and preferences of both small-scale retailers and larger consumers in the tomato industry. To promote recurring business, think about putting client loyalty programs into place. Establish direct means of communication as well, such as email campaigns or newsletters, to educate customers about new kinds, sales, and seasonal products. Building trust and loyalty with your clientele through active engagement can result in favorable word-of-mouth and long-term company success.

MARKETING TECHNIQUES

For your tomato business, effective promotional methods are essential to raising awareness and increasing sales. When tomatoes are in season, think about doing targeted campaigns or working with chefs and influencers to include your tomatoes in inventive recipes. Offering time-limited specials or bundling choices might draw interest as well. Share aesthetically appealing information on social media, like recipes, behind-the-scenes photos, and client endorsements. Events that are meant to promote your company, such as cooking demos or tastings, can further involve the community and leave a lasting impression.

A comprehensive strategy that includes branding, a clear marketing plan, balanced use of online and offline channels, the development of customer connections, and calculated promotional activities is necessary for successful marketing for a tomato company. Your tomato business may succeed in a cutthroat market and leave a lasting impact on clients by carefully handling these ideas.

CHAPTER EIGHT

REGULATORY AND LEGAL ASPECTS

COMPREHENDING AGRICULTURAL REGULATIONS

The procedures and activities that take place in the agricultural sector are mostly regulated by agricultural legislation. The purpose of these regulations is to guarantee the agricultural operations' sustainability, safety, and equity. They address many different topics, such as animal welfare, pesticide use, water management, and land use. To operate within the law and support the general well-being of the agriculture sector, farmers must possess a thorough awareness of these regulations.

LICENSES AND PERMITS

Getting all the licenses and permits required is a basic part of following agricultural laws. Depending on the type of agricultural activity—crop cultivation, livestock farming, or agro-processing, for example—these documents differ. It is up to farmers to negotiate the regulatory maze and obtain the necessary permits for their business. To obtain and maintain the appropriate permissions and licenses, this procedure includes comprehending the precise requirements specified by regulatory organizations, submitting the required paperwork, and making sure that all legal requirements are met.

ADHERENCE TO ENVIRONMENTAL GUIDELINES

The environment is greatly impacted by agricultural activities, including biodiversity, water quality, and soil health. Adherence to environmental regulations is essential for reducing adverse impacts and advancing sustainable agriculture. To reduce environmental degradation, rules covering things like garbage disposal, conservation techniques, and the usage of pesticides and fertilizers are in place. To make sure their activities comply with legal requirements and support long-term environmental sustainability, farmers must embrace eco-friendly approaches, put best practices into place, and keep up with changing environmental standards.

RISK MANAGEMENT AND INSURANCE

The agricultural industry is susceptible to several hazards by nature, such as weather-related incidents, crop diseases, and changes in the market. For farmers, risk management and insurance are essential parts of a comprehensive legal strategy. Agricultural insurance helps farmers recover and continue their operations by offering financial protection against losses brought on by unanticipated circumstances. Farmers must negotiate the inherent risks of agriculture while adhering to legal requirements by understanding the terms and conditions of insurance policies and investigating risk reduction measures.

FARMERS' LEGAL PROTECTIONS

Legal safeguards are necessary to protect farmers' interests and means of subsistence. Property rights, contracts, and laws ensuring equitable treatment and market access are a few examples of these protections. Farmers especially depend on property rights because they provide boundaries for their land use and offer security. To clearly define expectations and obligations, contracts with suppliers, buyers, and other stakeholders need to be carefully drafted. Furthermore, fair trade policies and market competitiveness are addressed by legislative frameworks, which help to establish a fair environment in which farmers can prosper.

For farmers to succeed and operate sustainably, they must understand the legal and regulatory environment. A comprehensive approach that guarantees the long-term profitability of agricultural activities must include understanding agricultural legislation, getting permissions and licenses, adhering to environmental standards, controlling risks through insurance, and taking advantage of legal safeguards.

CHAPTER NINE

CASE STUDIES AND STORIES OF TRIUMPH

ANALYZING PROFITABLE TOMATO FARMING ENTERPRISES

Examining the realm of prosperous tomato-growing companies reveals that several elements play a role in their success. The adoption of contemporary agriculture technology and techniques is one important factor. To maximize productivity and quality, successful farmers frequently use greenhouse cultivation, precision farming methods, and sophisticated irrigation systems. Furthermore, incorporating sustainable farming practices guarantees the business's long-term survival while also appealing to environmentally sensitive customers.

Effective supply chain management is a key component of tomato farming firms' success, even in the absence of technology. It is essential to have strong partnerships with retailers, distributors, and even direct-to-consumer channels. This gives producers more control over price and brand positioning in addition to guaranteeing a stable market. Building strong networks within the agricultural ecosystem is a top priority for successful farmers since it fosters collaborations that are advantageous to the farmer as well as the larger community.

ACQUIRING KNOWLEDGE FROM OBSTACLES AND SETBACKS

The agricultural sector is rife with difficulties and setbacks, and tomato cultivation is no exception. Sustained success requires an understanding of these obstacles and the ability to learn from them. Tomato growers frequently deal with a variety of issues, such as volatile markets, pest infestations, and changing weather. Successful farmers have learned to adapt and use resilient strategies when faced with challenges.

When mistakes are made, they can teach us important lessons. Farmers who have experienced losses frequently stress the value of variety in terms of income sources and crops. This not only offers different revenue streams during hard seasons, but it also lessens the effects of crop-specific difficulties. In addition, adopting ongoing education via workshops, peer-to-peer information sharing, and agricultural extension services is crucial for overcoming challenges.

MODIFYING TECHNIQUES FOR VARIOUS LOCATIONS

With varied climates, soil types, and market demands across different countries, tomato farming is a diversified operation. Successful farmers understand how important it is to modify their tactics to fit the unique circumstances of their region. Adopting drought-resistant tomato varieties and water-efficient irrigation techniques is crucial in areas with arid temperatures, for instance.

In the same vein, knowing the tastes of the local market and modifying agricultural techniques appropriately guarantees a more accommodating customer base.

Furthermore, productive tomato growers show a readiness to try out new cultivating methods and tomato varieties. This flexibility puts the farm in a position to profit from new market trends while also optimizing yield. Farmers can obtain important information on best practices unique to their region by working with researchers and interacting with their local agricultural extension agencies.

CONVERSATIONS WITH SKILLED TOMATO GROWERS

Interviews with seasoned tomato growers provided insights into their strategies and practical knowledge, which in turn contributed to their success. Many stress the value of lifelong learning and keeping up with business trends. These farmers frequently emphasize the need for mentoring, experience-sharing, and helping the upcoming crop generation.

The importance of ecologically friendly and sustainable methods keeps coming up in these interviews. Tomato farmers with experience often talk about using natural pest management, conserving soil, and implementing organic growing practices. This builds a robust and long-lasting farming paradigm in addition to meeting the growing demand from consumers for environmentally friendly produce.

A comprehensive strategy that incorporates supply chain management, technological innovation, and sustainable practices is revealed by looking at prosperous tomato-growing enterprises. The path to a successful and long-lasting tomato farming business includes learning from mistakes and setbacks, customizing tactics for different geographical areas, and utilizing the wisdom of seasoned farmers.

www.ingramcontent.com/pod-product-compliance
Lightning Source LLC
Chambersburg PA
CBHW050832290526
45792CB00001B/355